MORE SAX STORIES

TALES FROM EAST SUFFOLK

First published 2020
Copyright © 2020 by Belinda Moore

The moral right of the author has been asserted. No part of this book may be used or reproduced in any manner whatsoever without written permission of the author except in the case of quotations in reviews.

Design and typography, propellerdesign.co.uk
All photographs provided by the interviewees.

Front cover: Christine Mattinson on the rollercoaster at Saxmundham carnival around 1952.

"Life is not measured by the time we live."

George Crabbe

For my mother,
Sandra Moore

Contents

Introduction	9
Michael Adlam	10
Manette Baillie	18
Sybil Coxage	24
Philip Hope Cobbold	28
Robin Graham	34
Colin Hostler and Lyn Hostler	42
William Last	46
Christine Mattinson	50
Betty Noy	56
Acknowledgements	60

Introduction

It is autumn 1998 and I am sitting in the sunshine on a bench outside Kelsale club with Bill Last. Having a yarn, talking about his growing up in that very place. Laughing.

I recorded my conversation with Bill for the oral history archive at Saxmundham Museum. I wanted to preserve not only what he said but how he said it. Accents and phraseology change faster than you think. You have to get up pretty early these days to find Suffolk people who speak as once they did.

My plan here was to write fewer and more detailed stories than those that had featured in Sax Stories five years earlier. I completed a handful over 2018 and 2019. I was happy to go steady, choosing subjects carefully and taking time to listen to them.

Late 2019. Nearly there, I thought. And then 2020 fell upon us. In a moment, I had no access to the people to whom I hoped to listen. People died. Writing anything seemed impossible. The book felt hopeless.

I reviewed the stories that I had written and saw that, in addition to recording worlds that no longer exist, many demonstrate Suffolk people's determination to overcome adversity and to build lives in circumstances that many would find overwhelming. They are about getting on, making do, never complaining, making the best of what's thrown at you. I would follow their lead.

Each of the people featured here has a relationship with Saxmundham. Each story also has a slant towards agriculture and farming. It's fundamental to us, it's what made Saxmundham and it's what's changed our part of the world entirely in little over a generation.

There is no point pretending that 2020 isn't a vile year. Despite that, I have enormous gratitude for the stories that I did hear. I'm extremely lucky to have spent time with such interesting people.

Mike Adlam at the bullock building, Park Gate Farm, 1970s

Michael Adlam b.1934

'My father thought I was crazy wanting to farm rather than work in the family haulage business but I'd never wanted to do anything else.'

Mike Adlam had wanted to farm since he was a boy. His only experience was holiday work driving tractors for a local farmer when he was about 13,

'The farmer said he'd pay me what he thought I was worth. Everyone filed past the office window on a Friday to get paid and when he got to my turn, he looked at me and said, "I think this week you owe me!"

'I took the last school certificate in 1950, then went on to do A-Levels and eventually got a place at Reading University to study agriculture. Because I didn't come from farming stock, I had to do a year on a farm before I went to university.

'My year was in Burnham Market, Norfolk. It was absolutely superb, the best year of my life, really. Burnham Market was still very much a village then, compared to what it is now. To my mind, that whole coast has become Chelsea-ised, like Aldeburgh and Southwold.'

Mike Adlam was put to work on a farm of 1,400 acres which employed 40 men. It was part of the Holkham Estate.

'I stayed with the farm manager, Ernest Williamson. The owner, Brian Case, lived at Bingham and was a proper Norfolk gentleman. He hunted two days a week, shot two days a week and farmed on Fridays.'

In the 1950s, the East Anglian countryside appears to have been close-packed with characters. Men who had returned from war and those who had never left because agricultural work was a reserved occupation, essential to the national effort, and who, as a result, frequently occupied the same cluster of acres all their lives.

'The farm foreman was a character. He'd been on the farm since he was a boy and worked his way up through horseman and so on, ending up managing 40 men. He wasn't a great one for reading or writing but he was as smart as anything. Never forgot a thing. Mind you, If he fell out with someone, he sacked them, just like that.'

The farm had two herds of cows and 300 pedigree Oxford Down sheep. They also grew vegetables, farmed by hand.

'The sugarbeet alone took 12 men, all on piece work. They started at the end of September and that's all they did until Christmas; it was hard work but it was popular because it was good money.'

After the year at Burnham, Mike returned to Reading.

'I went home for a few months to help because my mother was ill, then I joined the army for National Service in 1957. I went into the Royal Engineers – I wanted to go to sea but the navy wouldn't take national servicemen – they'd had enough of them.

'After basic training, I was immediately posted to Singapore. There were two weeks before we left and, as mother had died, I applied for a compassionate posting because I worried that father might struggle. The army ignored the request and off I went.'

In 1957, Singapore was still effectively an active service posting.

'We took 100ft vessels up and down the coast to rescue troops from the so-called emergency.'

After a year, Mike returned home by boat, enjoying a week's leave in Hong Kong before stop-overs in Gibraltar, Aden and Colombo.

Mike wrote to Brian Case, the owner of the farm in Burnham where he'd spent a year, asking for advice about what he should do next.

'He suggested that I went to a farm in Filby, Norfolk, just north of Yarmouth. The farmer was an incredible man called Charlie Wharton. He could barely read or write and had started his business with the milk contract for Yarmouth hospital – ending up with 2,000 acres. An amazing brain; never forgot anything. He only had around 15 men, with two herds of cows, pigs and poultry. I went there as livestock foreman. His daughter ran the poultry unit.

'Charlie Wharton used to play bridge for Norfolk. He was a big bloke, about 6'3" and 17 or 18 stone and his bridge partner was Lord Walpole, who was a little man of about five foot nothing'

It was while Mike was working at Filby that he met his future wife, Diana Moore, at Young Farmers.

'Her father had a small tenant farm nearby. Charlie offered us a house so that I could stay working on the farm but Di was keen to get away.'

Mike took a farm manager's job in Swainsthorpe, managing 150 acres and a couple of men for a retired surgeon called Burfield.

'I'd seen a farm manager's job at Glemham Hall advertised in Farmer's Weekly. Flicks were controlling it and they asked me to come for an interview. They gave me a map of the farm and said to go and have a look round before my interview that afternoon. I wasn't over-impressed. It was pretty run-down. The Cobbold family had recently appointed Flicks to do something with it as they were losing money.'

As Mike walked round the farm that morning, he spotted two other men who appeared also to be candidates for the farm manager's job.

'I thought they looked about twice as old as me; I was only 27. I was sure I wouldn't get the job. In my interview, Tony Flick sat in the corner taking notes while his father asked the questions. The last question he asked was, "if you were going to take this farm as a tenant, what rent would you offer me?"

'I thought, "Christ, that's a stinker!" I think I said "about £3 an acre". When I got home, I said to Di, "well, I definitely didn't get that one." The next morning, Flick called to say that I'd got the job, if I still wanted it.'

At the time of Mike's appointment, there was a manager living in Peartree Farm, across the road from Glemham Hall.

'Flicks told the farm manager that he'd had too many men, I think he had five at the time for 300 acres. I think it was father Flick that put the boot in. He told him to get rid of some men and gave him a month to sort it out. When he went back a month later and asked who he would get rid of, the farm manager said that he couldn't do without any of them and Sam Flick said, "right, we'll manage without you." He was fair but straight to the point.'

Mike spent his first week staying in the White Hart in Saxmundham while Blaxhall Hall was made ready.

'When they told me that I'd got the job, Flicks said that Lady Cobbold would like to meet me. Di and I came down, banged on the door of the Hall and the door was opened by what I thought was the housekeeper and it turned out to be Lady Blanche.

'I got on with her ok. She had four children, John, who lived at Trimley and ran the Brewery, Patrick, the younger son, lived at home. Of the two daughters, Pam Carduggan had married twice and lived at Easton, and the other, Jean, was married to Roger Paul. Lady B lived in the Hall basically on her own. Her husband, Colonel John, known as Ivan, was killed in the Guards' Chapel when it was bombed in 1944.'

The farm at Glemham Hall had become very run-down and one of Mike's first tasks was to buy machinery. Flicks had told him that there was no money to spare and that he'd have to start from scratch.

'It was the shocking winter of '63, which wasn't a good start.'

According to the Met Office, the winter of 1963 was the coldest for more than 200 years. Around parts of the UK, the sea in harbours froze. A blizzard ripped across the country between Christmas and new year leaving a deep covering of snow which in some places, lasted until March. Farms were cut off, vegetable crops wasted, livestock starved.

'I bought a tractor and a plough, which I got a rocket for. Tony Flick was running it with Sam, keeping an eye over us. I'd go into Flicks office every week and collect the wages. The following year, Sam called me into his office (I thought "Oh Lord!") and said that Mr Hurran was leaving Parkgate Farm and did we want it. "You can't have both because we're going to have to let Blaxhall Hall." John Kerr was taking the tenancy.

'Parkgate House was in a pretty poor state. We were due to move on Michaelmas Day in '63. Our son Simon was two and David was very much on the way. David was born in the October of '63 at the Phyllis Memorial at Melton; we moved about a fortnight later. We were in the middle of moving and Dr John [Ryder Richardson] came over to have a look at the new baby. There were packing cases everywhere and for a good few minutes none of us could find him!'

The new tenancy meant that the Glemham Estate lost 300 acres and gained 500 including the parkland.

'The land I gained was better and responded to action pretty quickly. We started buying young cattle because we didn't have much capital. One day, a bull belonging to Jimmy Blyth from next door got out and bullied a couple of my young cows. It set my mind running and we started developing the farm deliberately buying heifer calves to graze the park. Martin Greenfield used to rent the far part and graze some milkers on it. As I built up cattle numbers, I began to take the park back. In the end we had 150 cows.'

Mike usually took the fat cows to the market in Saxmundham himself, hooking the cattle trailer up to a Land Rover.

'Tony Flick was one of the auctioneers and you always had a good day out on sale day.'

Next, the estate took Moat Farm and Peartree Farm back in hand, adding around 200 acres.

'Each time I started to think that we were beginning to get it sorted, more land came in. When Lord Alistair Graham, who had been tenant at Hill Farm, Farnham, died, I took that back in hand. There were no ingoings at all, which told me that his manager hadn't been doing the best job. It was sand land with some nice marshes. It suited me very well. We used to grow sugar beet and irrigate where we could. It turned out to be an ideal wintering ground for our cows. They never came in all year round.

'We added a few bits and pieces of land from the other side of the A12 and we took those and Grove Farm back when Robert Noy decided just to farm his own land.

'How things change over the years. Every time we took on more land, we just bought a bigger machine. In my student days in Norfolk, we had 40 men for a farm of 1,400 acres, by the time I retired in 1999, I was running the same size farm with 400 cattle and just five men.'

When Mike retired, the land at Glemham was out to contract and initially Kerrs took it on. Today, it's farmed by Bill Kemball from Wantensden Farms. Mike's younger son works for him.

Farm managers rarely own their own home. Fortunately, Mike and Diana had bought a house in Melton and let it out to American servicemen. Tenants eventually bought the house.

'Smithy, who used to work for Flicks, helped us start looking in Sax,

Wickham Market, Fram. Eventually, they called to say that they thought they'd found a house for us. At that point, in 1998, this place [on Street Farm Road] was surrounded by fields.'

WREN Manette Baillie 1942

Manette Baillie b.1922

A friend tipped me off about Manette. 'You have to talk to Manette in Benhall, she's 97, still plays bridge, amazing woman, you'll love her.' When I arrived to interview her, I assumed that the person who opened the door to me was a much younger helper. Of course not. Manette, having come in from pruning in the garden, baking a ginger cake and was doing her email. After listening to her story, what struck me most was her eloquence and humour. She is very clever, very witty. She faces the future not the past.

'We spoke French at home. My mother was French and she'd met my English father when he was studying at university in Lille before the First World War. He was a remarkable man. He could speak French without a discernible English accent.'

Manette left school in July 1939 when Britain was preparing for war. It wasn't officially declared until September. Sixteen-year-old Manette joined the Women's Land Army which had been established during the First Word War and re-formed at the start of the Second World War. Land Girls came from all walks of life and were intended to replace male farm workers who had gone to war.

'I was sent to Devon and I loved it. I was hidden away with a nice farming family with four daughters. There was no mains water and no electricity but I learned how to milk a cow and how to use the milking equipment when that arrived.

'One day, when the farmer was going out, he told me to let the cows out and turn the bull into its field. I tried, but the bull wouldn't stop following me. In the end, I shut myself in one of the stalls until the bull lost interest.

'My sister was in London with a new baby and her husband had gone to war. He wanted his wife and baby to be evacuated so they were sent down to Devon to be with me. It was a disaster. We were all sharing rooms of course and the baby would wake in the night and I needed to be up and starting work at 5 am.

'My sister was very unhappy and decided to return to London. She wanted me to accompany her. My father insisted that I return too and continue my education. I went back to college to study shorthand-typing like all young women in those days. If you didn't have shorthand-typing, you couldn't earn a living. We did things like economics too.'

Manette took a job at Wandsworth town hall. The building was hit by a bomb and badly damaged. Fortunately, it happened at night while it was unoccupied.

'In 1940, I joined the WRENS. I worked as a shorthand-typist at Fulham Gas Works where young men were being trained to be aircraft fitters. I never set foot on a boat! My boss had been a pilot in the First World War and couldn't get over not being able to fly. It was quite sad to see him staring out the window at the planes.'

Manette volunteered to work abroad and in 1942 was one of 60 WRENS who set sail for Durban, South Africa as part of a convoy of ships from Liverpool.

'The storm in the Bay of Biscay was so bad, we could see the propeller rising up on the ship in front of us. We could hear an army band playing and joked that we could be on the Titanic. It took us six weeks to get to Durban. When we arrived in January, the lights were on but within 24 hours, a blackout was declared.'

Durban was the centre for naval movement control at the time when the allied forces could not use the Mediterranean. It provided a stopping-off point for hundreds of convoys with troops en route to deployment. Manette was stationed in Durban for a year until the Mediterranean reopened and all allied troops were moved from South Africa. Manette worked in Cairo then Alexandria before arriving in Port Said to complete her two year posting. She was made a Petty Officer before sailing back to the UK in 1944 for two week's leave with her family in London.

'My parents had had to put up with the Blitz and large parts of London being blown to pieces. It seemed like there were doodlebugs coming over all the time. I expect they had a worse war than I did, really.'

It was at Weymouth Naval Base in 1945 that Manette met, got engaged to and then married war hero Derek Bowden. They were both 23. Bowden was a dashing and handsome army officer who had already built a reputation for daring.

In 1941, Bowden had led a British Army charge on horseback against Vichy-controlled forces in Syria. His troops wore red capes and carried First World War rifles and sabres. He was badly wounded and taken to a Jerusalem hospital, where he became enthralled by the Israeli state and engaged to a Jewish girl. When discharged he volunteered for the British Parachute Brigade near the Suez Canal, then fought in Sicily, Italy and on D-Day with the SAS. In September 1944 he was parachuted into the Battle of Arnhem where he was badly injured and sent to a POW camp from where he escaped only to be recaptured. As a punishment, he was sent to work as a labourer at the Bergen-Belsen concentration camp, carrying corpses from living quarters. He was eventually discharged from a prison camp near Hanover.

'Understandably he never got over the Belsen experience. He had been scarred by so many events in the war that civilian life was impossible. We stayed with my parents and then got a prefab house at Morden in what was grimly called the Gravel Pits Estate. Within nine months of our marriage, our son Anthony had arrived but Derek had no work. The marriage was a disaster and lasted only two years.'

Manette wrote to her sister, Thérèse, who was living in Switzerland, offering to be her au pair. Bowden went to Yugoslavia to work as a parachute instructor and then on to Israel where he fought with distinction in the Israeli war against Palestine.

'My sister lived in Chur, a medieval city in the Rhine valley, with her Swiss teacher husband, their four children and a fifth one on the way. She also took in boarders and a couple of orphaned German schoolboys. I came over on the train with Anthony, who was just two years old. Then I managed to make a difficult situation worse by getting appendicitis. I was in hospital and my sister now had five young children to look after – there was a fantastic amount of cleaning and cooking to do and she was much more interested in intellectual topics like history and religion. I don't know how she did it. Fortunately, my brother in England heard about our predicament and sent the money to pay for the hospital bill.

'I'd been writing to a man that I'd met in Port Said. After some time, he wrote to me from India asking me to marry him. Adam Reid Baillie, always known as Reid, was an ex Royal Navy Volunteer Reserve. He was already 30 when the war started – too old to be a pilot in the RAF, which had been his dream. Instead, he was sent on the Arctic Convoys as an Able Seaman. It was a terrible experience which scarred him for life.

'Reid was happy to adopt Anthony and initially we settled in Bath. I didn't want to go anywhere that was more than 100 miles from London. Reid took over a hay, straw and corn merchant without knowing anything about hay, straw or corn. Remarkably, we made it work, essentially by putting time and effort in and being prepared to go out of our way to help people.'

Reid's habit of investing in businesses of which he had little or no knowledge continued with a garden supplies firm and then a farm in the Cotswolds.

'My short experience as a Land Girl was all we knew of farming yet he decided to buy a 200-acre farm in the Cotswolds. It was a very, very beautiful spot with a house a mile down a lane. We had to buy a house cow. The land was very hilly, not quite steep enough to be classified as a hill farm and we bought nine elderly sheep at auction.

'Even though we never made any money and were really farming from a book, it was such a lovely place, my family came to stay all the time. When Reid wanted to leave after five years – all his business projects lasted five years – I didn't want to go. I was so happy there, I had horses and could go riding, the area was unbelievably beautiful. The local people had been marvellous to us, helping in any way they could. We were one of the last true family farms in the Cotswolds.'

It was the 1950s and Reid Baillie was in his late 40s. He decided that he was getting too old for such active farming and invested in a business selling organic seeds mail-order based in the centre of Bristol.

'He always thought that the next place would be better than the last.'

While they were there, Reid spotted an article in the paper about Benhall in Suffolk and in particular a house called Limetree House, an impressive six-bedroom family home. He visited it on his own to have a look, fell in love with the house and in 1961 decided that they had to move there.

'When I came to have a look with my mother, I remember she said, "how will you make new friends?" The locals weren't outgoing and for some time it was as if no one would speak to us, but we brought the organic seed mail-order business with us and we soon got to know people by offering part-time work. The business was based in the house and garage.'

In 1970, tragedy struck. Anthony, by then a handsome 23-year-old, broke his neck diving off a promenade into the sea and was left paraplegic.

'There are no words. Anthony wanted to live and eventually established a full and happy life for himself, living in Norwich, working as an accountant. He fell in love with his carer and they became partners. He remained in contact with his father, Derek Bowden, and was close to his half-brothers and -sisters which was nice for all of them. I was fortunate enough to be able to build a suitable house in Benhall in which he could spend his later years. He lived until 70 and never once complained about his situation.'

Manette had moved into the house across the road from Limetree House when a friend had bequeathed her the property. It was the place that had provided the space to build the wheelchair-accessible house for Anthony, but Reid, who loved Limetree, refused to move.

'We got on well, I had my space and he had his. He would come for lunch every day and we would play bridge and socialise together. It was a happy arrangement for all concerned.'

One day, he didn't turn up for lunch and Manette found him ill, by himself at Limetree. The shock made him decide to join her over the road. Reid died in 1995.

In 1997, Anthony's father, Derek Bowden, came to visit.

'I married him again, hoping it would last longer than the first time, but no. It was disastrous. I went to live on his farm in Norfolk but I couldn't get back to Benhall quickly enough. And of course I missed Saxmundham, "the hub of the universe" where everyone headed for the weekly cattle market and auction run by Tony Flick. Alas! All now has been replaced by supermarkets. But time must march on.'

Manette continues to live in Benhall in the house opposite Limetree. She is enormously active in the life of the village, supporting others, continuing to play bridge, her opinion of East Anglians having changed to one of love and admiration.

Sybil Coxage

Sybil Coxage b.1931

Sybil Coxage spent her early years living on the family farm in East Green, near Kelsale. She is the youngest of six children, with five older brothers.

'We had a small dairy herd of about 10 cows and my father, William Friend, delivered milk to Saxmundham. There were no tractors in those days. The farm had working horses and my father would trim them up and take them to the Suffolk Show. We had to walk to Kelsale to go to the school there.

'When I was 10, we moved to Valley Farm at Snape and my eldest brother joined the navy. I liked being at the school in Snape and got top marks for writing but Mr Watkins, the headmaster, wasn't a nice man.

'I remember that we knitted gloves and socks for the war effort. The cemetery at Snape was just across the road and used to be full of mushrooms which we picked and sold.

'I was 13 when I left school because my birthday fell in the summer. My dad died when I was 11. My brother Frank married Daphne Gillet and took over the farm. Mum and me and my other brothers then moved to a bungalow.

'I helped my mother at home and then, when I was 14, I got a job at Constances, an ironmongers in Aldeburgh. I used to cycle to Aldeburgh every day come rain or snow. Very occasionally, I'd get a lift from a man who worked at Reeds the builders in Aldeburgh and drove a truck there so he'd put my bike on the back.

'I loved the work there and it helped my maths because I'd have to work out the prices for the odd numbers of screws and nails that people bought. Being able to go for a walk along Cragg Path in my lunch break was a real treat.

'I married my husband Reg Coxage when I was 23. He was about six years older than me. He'd been part of the gang of men that used to come round and help the farmers – War Ag we called it. The demobbed men provided farmers with extra labour, helping with threshing and so on.'

Reg had been part of the convoys that had taken supplies to the north of Russia.

The Arctic Convoys, the first of which took place in 1941, carried supplies to the very north of what was then the Soviet Union. The British boats took the narrow passage between the Arctic ice pack and German bases in Norway to the ports of Murmansk and Archangel. It was incredibly dangerous and many of the convoys were attacked by German submarines, aircraft and warships.

'I don't think Reg ever got over how terrible the convoys were. They couldn't stop even to rescue their mates who had gone overboard after being hit by torpedoes.'

Thousands of men returned home from the Second World War having seen things that should never have been seen and done things that should never have been done. They were expected to integrate immediately back into normal life, becoming model husbands and fathers, productive members of the community. There was no formal psychological or emotional support. Although 'shell shock' was recognised as an unfortunate effect of combat in the First World War, it was assumed to be a short-lived condition. Post-Traumatic Stress Disorder (PTSD) wasn't officially diagnosed until after the Vietnam war in the 1970s and officially recognised as a condition (initially in the USA) until 1980. Discharged men were supposed only to be grateful to be home, to take comfort in their allotment or from a pint with their mates at the legion or the local pub. Wives were expected to manage the often life-long damage suffered by the men they had married. Of course, many never spoke about their experiences at all, holding in silence for ever or until a final opening back on their deathbeds.

'When Reg came back from Russia, he was moved from the navy to the army and sent to Ireland for training, somewhere they could get used to hills, then he went off to Rangoon in Burma. I still have his letters to his mum.

'In 1954, we moved into Park Road, Saxmundham. Reg was still working for the War Ag but then he got a job with the railway as a lengthsman, checking the lines, making repairs and so on. They worked on Sundays, replacing worn sleepers and repairing the lines.
'Our daughter Susan was born in 1964 and our son Peter in 1968.

'They were busy times. Reg used to grow our own veg and I'd go into Sax for the shopping at the International Stores and Clarkes. When we went out, it was to the British Legion in Albion Street. Reg was very involved with the Legion and was a standard-bearer for years.

'When the children were a little older I started work in the kitchen at the Middle School in Sax, working with Mrs Stone. Mr Rasmussen was the headmaster then – a very fair and genuine man.'

Philip Hope-Cobbold

Philip Hope-Cobbold b.1943 – d.2020

'I was born in 1943, at Glemham Hall. My mother was Pamela Cobbold and my father South African, of Scottish extraction. He was serving in the Grenadier Guards over here in the war. I started life as a Hope-Johnstone, my father's name.

'My mother was in the ATS [Auxiliary Territorial Service, the women's branch of the British Army during the Second World War] and that's how they met. They were only married for some six years.

'When I was born, my grandfather, Captain John Murray Cobbold, known as Ivan, was still alive. He bought Glemham Hall in 1923 and moved here from Holywells in Ipswich with his wife, Lady Blanche.

'Ipswich was forever expanding and my young grandfather obviously thought that, "here's a chance to get out of town", so he bought the Glemham Hall estate.

'Of course when I was born, it was wartime and this was quite a handy spot. When my mother had left the ATS, it was fairly safe living here with her family. The house wasn't filled with troops but had a lot of medical equipment in it.

'I lived here until about 1946 when my father got a job with the British Embassy or British Council in Holland, so we went to live there until around 1949. I do remember being in Holland although I was a young child. Of course it was just after the war and Holland was recovering from occupation and everything else that had gone on there, but I remember enjoying it. My father worked in the Hague, which is where I think the British Embassy was then, and we lived in Wassenaar and then moved to a country house, château-type place called De Harte Kampe.

'At that age, you pick up languages very easily although I don't remember it now. I remember trying to teach the gardener a little bit of English. My brother Charles was born in 1948.

'My parents' marriage sadly went up the creek around 1949 and my mother, my brother and I returned here to Glemham Hall.

'My grandfather Ivan had been killed in 1944 when a flying bomb destroyed the Guards' Chapel in London. He was a captain in the First

World War and had become a Colonel in the Second World War.

'Between times, he had returned to be Chairman of Cobbold Brewing, which left my grandmother, Lady Blanche, who was a daughter of the 9th Duke of Devonshire, here with her other daughter, Jean, and two sons, John and Patrick Cobbold. My mother was their elder sister.

'My mother bought a house near Framlingham and I lived there from about 1950 until about 1960. She had two young children and I imagine she wanted a little independence. While we lived at Fram, I attended Fairfield School in Sax with Miss Partridge and Miss Farthing. I came into Sax by bus from Fram every morning and back in the evening. I enjoyed it, there are a lot of people from around here who went there.

'After Framlingham, we moved to Easton, again only a few miles from Little Glemham and she lived there until she died in 1994.

'After Fairfield, I went to King's College Choir School in Cambridge. I think my mother chose that school for me because she was persuaded by Benjamin Britten. They were friends and he delivered me for my first term at King's in either a Bentley or a Rolls Royce with a soft-top roof, if I remember rightly.

'I enjoyed being at the choir school but I sometimes think that, being a country boy, I might have been better off somewhere else. Cambridge was full of the sons of intellectuals and seemed very "proper" after a country childhood. Our headmaster was an ex-wartime bomber pilot who kept a firm grip on the place.

'I remember that I got on very well with the handyman. Because I'd grown up in the country, I knew how to work mowing machines and so on and used to help mow the cricket pitches and other things like that.

'I went from Kings to Radley College near Oxford. I really followed the headmaster who was lined up to be my housemaster at Eton. He'd been in the army with my father in the war and was a family friend. When he became the headmaster at Radley, he took a gang of us with him, including me, which was useful for my mother because when she visited, she could stay with the headmaster and his family.

'I left Radley at 18 and had started helping out during school holidays on a farm of a retired general, Major General Charles Miller at Badingham, who, after I'd worked there, asked if I'd consider joining the army and his regiment.

'I went to Sandhurst in 1963 and did two years there, which is what you did in those days, and passed out as the Senior Under Officer of the Sovereign's Company. We won all the prizes that year. I also spent a couple of months on exchange at West Point Military Academy in the USA.

'I joined the 13th/18th Royal Hussars (Queen Mary's Own) and I served in that regiment from 1964 to 1992. It took me to BAOR (British Army of the Rhine), Northern Ireland – several tours, Malaya, Canada and Oman.

'I married my first wife, Jay, in 1968 and had two sons, Tom and Tim. We sadly divorced in 1983.

'When I left the army in 1992, I lived in London and worked as a hotel and restaurant inspector for the RAC. I travelled around the country looking at hotels and restaurants that had paid to have an inspector visit incognito – an odd system. Generally, I covered the London area and south of London, right down to the Isle of Wight.

'I was living in a small flat in Tooting when my uncle Patrick Cobbold died in 1994. His elder brother John had died in 1983 and their mother, Lady Blanche, had died here at Glemham in 1987. She was elderly by then and had been ill – seeing the devastation brought about by the gales of 1987 was the final blow for her.

'Patrick was only nine years older than me so I had always assumed that if he died when he was elderly, I would myself be getting on and there wouldn't be much point in starting here in my 70s or 80s. I presumed that he and I would move on at roughly the same time and that he would leave the estate to the next generation, which may have been my eldest son.

'However, he died in his 60th year – the same year that my mother died. I was sitting in my flat in Tooting when I got a telephone call and a telegram. I was quite surprised.

'In many ways, I felt like I was coming home to Suffolk. My parents had divorced in the 1950s so my whole life was around here: Easton, Framlingham, Little Glemham. I'd go beating with the keepers, I knew the farms and the house, it felt natural to come back.

'I thought, well, I need "Hope", but I'll change the last part of my name to Cobbold as I was returning to that part of my family. My father had gone back to South Africa and I never had much communication with him until his latter years. Everyone agreed that I could happily change my name from Hope-Johnstone to Hope-Cobbold.

'When I took over, the estate had around 2,800 acres although some of it has since been sold off. It's a big responsibility to take on – it took ten years to pay the death duties!

'In 1995, I became a director of Ipswich Town Football Club, the club that had been started as a professional club by my grandfather in 1936. John and Patrick Cobbold, my uncles, had both been chairman.

'I had always followed the team. When Ipswich won the FA cup in 1978, I watched that with a friend of mine, consuming a large bottle of South African dry sherry, sitting in a grotty old hut while stationed in Northern Ireland on military duty. Being involved with the club was good fun. I'm no longer a director because the old guard sold up in 2007, but I am now a patron of ITFC. Around 2005, I became Deputy Lieutenant of Suffolk and then High Sheriff of Suffolk.

'In 2002, I married again, to Raewyn who had come originally from New Zealand but was settled in Suffolk running a bed and breakfast at Pipp's Ford near Needham Market. She sadly died in 2016.

'When Saxmundham Museum started in 2001, Richard Crisp and Helen Revell approached me, I can't remember exactly when – probably when I was popping into Richard's shop in the High Street.

'It's always been a very jolly thing to do, with gatherings a couple of times a year and an excellent collection of interesting people.'

Major Philip Hope-Cobbold had been President of Saxmundham Museum since the museum's foundation.

His support continually went above and beyond what might be expected of someone in that role. He attended management meetings and AGMs, friends' events and social functions, and hosted friends' evenings at Glemham Hall.

Everyone involved with the museum was devastated to hear of his death in July 2020. His son, Tom, gave permission for this interview to be published.

Robin Graham during a trip to Albania,1960

Robin Graham b.1926

Robin Graham and I met when on the management committee of Saxmundham Museum. He was responsible for the museum's shop and a frequent and enthusiastic steward. His wit and intelligence belie his age and it was only when I got to know him a little better that I came to realise just how many lives he'd led.

Robin had sailed around wartime Britain as a teenage midshipman, run a small broiler farm near Vienna, worked as a social worker in some of the most challenging parts of London, and farmed in Blaxhall, not far from the place of his birth.

It was another museum occasion that I let slip to one of the guests that I hoped to interview Robin. The guest leant over and whispered very quietly that I should ask Robin about Princess Margaret. When the time came, I did. He laughed loud and long, 'that woman! in the 50s she was like my bete noire!'

When we reviewed the initial draft of this interview together, Robin's primary concern was that, if people knew of his aristocratic roots, they might think 'I'm one of those ghastly snobs.' Of course, If he were a ghastly snob, he would never be troubled by such a thought.

Robin Graham was born at Chantry Farm, Campsea Ashe, the youngest of four children of Lord Alastair Graham and Lady Meriel Bathurst. His uncle, James Graham, was the 6th Duke of Montrose, politician, founder of the Royal Navy Volunteer Reserve (RNVR) and inventor of the aircraft carrier. He was also profoundly deaf.

'We would often spend our holidays in Scotland,' says Robin, 'Uncle Jim was a very entertaining man. He was extremely deaf and used to have this device on the dining table that somehow helped him to hear. He'd tell funny stories and when he'd had enough, he'd simply turn his hearing device off.'

James Graham and his family owned the estate at Easton, near Wickham Market. When this was sold, Alastair Graham and his family moved to Chantry Farm at Campsea Ashe, where Robin and his siblings grew up. According to Robin, his uncle made the decision to sell without consulting his wife.

When Robin left school at Winchester College, Britain was at war.

'I had French and I was also studying Russian. I'd left school at Winchester in 1944, before I was 17, and won a place at Oxford in the Y scheme, which was designed to get people into the services who might become officers.'

Instead, his college was taken over by the army and in 1944, Robin began naval training, just a few weeks after his 18th birthday.

'We were sent to Oxford where we rowed whalers down the river and back, ferrying Petty Officers to and from their ships; learning our bends and hitches, Morse code, that kind of thing. We were all together and it was fun, there wasn't a lot of drink about because of rationing at the end of the war, but we managed to get some cider.'

After six months, he was moved to HMS Raleigh, the navy's training base near Plymouth, 'I remember wonderful weather, it was May, there was lots and lots of cider and free time sitting under apple trees in local pub gardens. The view of Mount Edgcumbe House and its park was so wonderful, it could be very hard to concentrate when doing drill.'

Robin's training group was then tasked with taking one of two old cruisers, HMS Dauntless, around Britain in June.

'It was wonderful, we anchored ourselves at various points and let ourselves down on planks. There were about 30 of us, we slept in hammocks and spent our days scrubbing decks and ironing uniforms.

'After that we were sent to Hove and stayed in an old swimming pool under a car park. It smelled ghastly, of cement, like sleeping in the air raid shelter at school.'

The midshipmen were in Plymouth when news of VE Day, the end of the Second World War in Europe, came through.

'We celebrated in Plymouth Hoe where Lady Astor had a house. She had been very anti-drink but ended the evening with a drunken sailor on each arm!'

Nancy Astor, Viscountess Astor, was the first woman MP to take a seat, after she won the Plymouth Sutton constituency in 1919.

At 19, Robin Graham ended his Royal Navy training as a midshipman. He spent a further two years in the service, running crew back and forth off the Queen Elizabeth dreadnought battleship, wasting time in Londonderry, learning to dive.

'The full diving kit in those days included a very heavy steel helmet and leather boots. We brought ourselves up by putting our fingers over the valve in the neck which let air out. There were two of us on the course and my colleague always blew himself up like a Michelin man and had to be hauled in like a fish!'

He completed his service with the Royal Navy in November 1947, age 21, a Sub-Lieutenant at last. Robin took a holiday with his sister, Lilias, who had been working with refugees in Austria.

'We met in Switzerland and had a wonderful time. There was no rationing.'

Returning to the UK, he began a year as a farm worker in Norfolk.

'I was put up with a family in an old rectory full of very odd people. The daughter of the house had been an ATS officer in the war and always made toast that tasted of paraffin - there was no electricity. I was expected to take her to dances.'

He then began a three-year agricultural course at Cambridge University.

'I thought it was a complete waste of time because the University didn't have a farm of its own. After the first year out of town, my next was in Trinity Street and the final year in college, completely the wrong way round! I had enjoyed Oxford much more than Cambridge.'

Back in Suffolk, he had second thoughts about going straight back to working on a farm.

'I decided that I was in danger of spending my entire life in the same small area of East Suffolk so I decided to go to Austria. My thought was that I'd get to see a lot of opera, ski a lot.'

Equipped with 'three words of German', he found a nice house about 20k outside Vienna.

'It was in Unteroberndorf, the first proper village outside Vienna, beyond suburbia. A farmer had an acre in front of the house, with one horse and one ox, there was a shop full of gossip, two pubs and a kiosk, smitten with flies, where the butcher set up shop. Along with the house came a Lloyd van, timber framed with a tiny motor the size of a mower motor, but it had enough room for my chickens.

'Much of my time was spent with English-speaking music students from the conservatoire in Vienna. Often, I'd have a houseful staying at the farm.'

Robin returned to England in 1962 and began a post-graduate course in social work at Exeter University. He worked in Plymouth for five years before moving to work for Tower Hamlets council in Waltham Forest for a further eight.

His social responsibilities were numerous.

'I was obliged to accompany Princess Margaret to the ballet at Covent Garden, along with a friend of course. This was just after the Townsend affair, and it seemed that I kept bumping into her.

'We were both guests at a wonderful lunch at Somerleyton. Our hosts had decided that we would have Sunday lunch on top of the tower; there was a small kitchen half way up, so it wasn't too inconvenient to serve. It was a glorious day, I will remember it always.

'The next day I was at a drinks party at Marlesford and Margaret was there and later, in London, I'd arrived early for a play at the Haymarket Theatre and was taking time to get some air when a large car pulled up next to me and out got Margaret followed by Roddy Llewellyn.'

Robin left his life as a social worker in London after receiving news that his father was ill and might only have six weeks left to live.

'I arrived back at Campsea Ashe to find that my father wasn't yet at death's door. He was frustrated at getting older because he'd always been active and interested in so many things. In fact, he went on to live for six months, rather than six weeks. He was 90 in May 1978 and passed away the following December.'

Robin set to work helping with the management of the farm and the maintenance of the house.

'I did an awful lot of painting and decorating because the house had fallen into disrepair.'

The farm, which had a small dairy herd and some pigs at Blaxhall, alongside around some 340 acres, had grown a number of debts.

'The farm lost a lot of money but eventually, I managed to separate the livestock from the arable and, by selling my flat in London, managed to make sure that the business was healthy.'

After Robin's father died, he took over the tenancy of Stone Farm Blaxhall, the location of a famous Suffolk legend.

The Blaxhall stone, a huge, smooth granite rock of about three tons, sits directly outside the back door of the farm house. Legend has it that the stone grows, and that it was placed there a century ago by a ploughman who had dug it up when it was the size of a loaf of bread.

'People would often stop and ask to see it," says Robin. 'There's a picture of it in the early editions of Ask the Fellows Who Cut The Hay. George Ewart Evans, the book's author, lived in the village and I knew him well. He used to ask me about certain Suffolk dialect words because he came from Wales and hadn't grown up hearing them.'

Six years after their father had died, Robin's older brother, Ian, returned to Chantry Farm from the USA, where he had spent more than 30 years working at Harvard University.

'After university, Ian worked as a picture restorer at the National Gallery. He bought this extravagantly designed open-topped Rolls Royce with a boat-shaped rear. He was convinced that he would be able to sell it in the west coast of America for a lot more than he'd paid, so he had it shipped out, and started out on an adventure, driving across the country from New York.

'Ian always said that the steering wheel was stuck turning left, because instead of California, he ended up in Mexico City. He went to the national museum and was entranced by the Mayan figures.'

Ian Graham is widely considered to be the world's leading authority on Mayan script, being the first person to transcribe and translate more than a tiny portion of it. He was awarded an OBE for his work alongside a Guatemalan honour and a Mexican honour and the MacArthur Fellowship at Harvard.

'When he did come home, it was quite obvious that there was something wrong,' says Robin.

Ian Graham was showing early signs of Alzheimer's disease, and although he managed to remain at Chantry Farm for five years, caring for him became increasingly challenging and in 2010 he moved to a nursing home.

When Robin eventually retired in 2003, he moved from Blaxhall to Saxmundham.

'I liked Saxmundham and thought that it would suit me if I needed to stop driving, it was a town with a station and only four miles from Blaxhall.

'I enjoyed stewarding at the museum, particularly when there were visitors with a connection to the area – it can be very interesting. I like the town but sometimes wonder where all the new house-building will end. Thank god they've built the skate park so that there's somewhere for the young people to go.'

Lyn and Colin Hostler in 1973 age 17

Colin Hostler and Lyn Hostler b.1956

Colin Hostler was born in Parham where his father worked on the farm. He has a younger brother, Christopher.

'When I was 17, I passed my driving test and was selling my moped. Lyn's dad brought her to Parham to have a look at it. She decided to buy it and that was it, really, we started going out after that!

'We lived on North Green Parham; the village has three greens. Mum worked for the farm too, I remember her repairing sacks with Copydex, hammering away at patches – not a nice job.

'It was a hard life for women in those days. She'd have to fetch the water for the house from a standpipe 200 yards away and heat it in a copper ready for the tin bath that went in front of the fire. Everyone shared the same water. My dad got in first and then my mum. By the time it got to me and my brother, the water was cloudy with coal tar soap. I hated it, it seemed that I'd come out dirtier than I got in. Our toilet was down the garden.

'We grew all our veg. I remember eating stinging nettles, cooked like spinach. If something hadn't grown well or you didn't have enough, the village would help out. We had chickens and a goat when I was young. Mum always said we were brought up on goat's milk.

'It was a very close community. I went to the village school; there were about 20 children altogether there. My father had been to that school too. At weekends and holidays, we'd play on the fields and on the airfield. There was a river in the village where we'd go to catch sticklebacks. We'd put them in jam jars.

'I was just seven when I helped dad mix the pig feed. He gave me a shilling every time I finished a batch and I saved up until I could buy a brand new watch from Kings Watchmaker in Framlingham. I've still got it.

'When I was about 11, I had to start helping my dad out on the farm. I learned to drive a tractor. It was a David Brown 25D, and the only way I could get the clutch to go down was to stand up on it because it was so stiff and I was so small. When I let it off, I could sit down. I would get in trouble with the farmer for stalling because things fell off the back of the trailer!

'I was the same age when I'd help out with the sugarbeet; a horrible cold job. They'd leave you in the middle of a 20-acre field and come back and get you at dinnertime.

'When I was 11, we had to leave Parham school and go to the Modern School in Fram [now called Thomas Mills]. I was leaving somewhere with 20 pupils and where I knew everyone, to a school with about 400 where I knew virtually no one. I don't think any of us liked it. There was just one girl that I knew and she still lives in the village. I did what I had to do to get through. The things I was interested in were cars and engineering.

'Before I went to Fram, I'd saved up so that I could buy a new bike to get to school on. It took about 20 minutes each way. The school did have bikes that people could borrow but they weren't very good. I was pleased to have one of my own.

'I left school at 15 and went to work at Marlesford Garage on the A12, where the Farm Shop and Café now is. I started off sweeping the floor, doing the odd jobs and listening and, by the time I was 17, I was doing breakdowns, welding, servicing cars, puncture repairs, fetching cars, selling petrol. I learned so much every day. I worked at the garage from 1971 to 1978. I did a milk round in Fram for a couple of weeks and then got a job for the council on the dust carts. It paid £48 per week, a big difference from the £28 per week I'd been earning at the garage! I stayed with that for 28 year; started off building big muscles lifting big heavy bins on my shoulders.'

Colin and Lyn got married in 1977 when they were 21. Lyn then moved to Parham.

Lyn Hostler grew up in Ardleigh near Colchester. 'My dad was a farmer and my mum worked on the land and then as a housekeeper. I have two brothers and a sister but they are all at least 10 years older than me.

'Ardleigh was a stretched-out village. We used to play outside, kicking footballs about, and help on the farm; we were very free. I started at Ardleigh Primary School which had 30 to 40 pupils and then we went on to Manningtree Secondary School which was much bigger and I didn't like it.

'I was nearly 16 when I left school and went to work in Woolworths in Colchester. From there I went to the Co-op and from there to Curtis's

Shoe Shop in Colchester, learning to measure people's feet. My last job out that way was at the VG Stores [a large grocery shop] in Colchester.

'When I was 16 and got Colin's old moped, I used to go to work on that. At 17, I passed my test and got a car.'

In 1978, Lyn and Colin's son Ronnie was born and in 1980, their son Danny arrived.

Lyn did a variety of farm work after the boys started school. 'I picked potatoes in Cransford, packed strawberries at Laxfield and beans in Leiston. It was all seasonal work. I think the worst was pulling the wild oats out of the corn because you got wet and it hurt your back. At the same time, I did some household jobs to earn some extra cash.'

The couple moved to Saxmundham in 1992, buying their house in Albion Street. Lyn worked for 14 years at the Gateway supermarket which became Somerfield and is now Waitrose.

'We'd had to leave Parham because the farmer wanted our house back,' says Colin. 'I'd always been to Sax and even as a boy, I would come with my dad to the livestock market.

'When we'd moved, I started Saxmundham Sports Model Club with Michael Emsden, who was at the time chairman of the main Saxmundham Sports Club. We flew model aeroplanes at Carlton Park. It became so popular that we ended up with 36 members.
'We stopped flying up there in 2000 because there were so many new houses being built and some people felt that they were being disturbed by the noise.

'Now I still make my models but I fly them at Parham, Phoenix club in Pakefield, and Gosbeck near Ipswich. Lyn always comes too. We also have some classic model boats and yachts and we sail those at the pond near Kingston Playing Field in Woodbridge.'

Each November, Colin comes out of retirement to start work as Father Christmas at the Red House Christmas Barn near Sternfield. 'I can see as many as 2,000 children over the course of the season. The most magical thing is seeing the excitement in their faces as they see Father Christmas sitting there waiting for them.'

William Last marries Barbara Mower, 1955

William Last b.1929

Bill Last was born in Aldeburgh. He was four when his family moved to Kelsale, near Saxmundham, in order that his mother could take up the post of crossing keeper.

'We moved to the East Green gatehouse. Father was a plate-layer on the Ipswich to Lowestoft line. It was hard manual work in those days. We lived by the railway so we'd see him and the other workers coming by most days.

'As a little boy it was exciting seeing the steam engines roaring by so close to the house; the sound of them would be enough to wake you up in the morning.'

Bill was one of six children, three boys and three girls. He went to the village school in Kelsale [now part of the village hall and social club] where there were four classrooms. The headmaster was Mr Bolton.

'They didn't think that I was very good at learning so I spent most of my time doing jobs in the garden and running errands.

'When I was about 13 and a half, I started working for Major Vaughan in North Green, milking the cows in the morning before school, that sort of thing. I left school when I was 14 and started working for him full-time on the farm.

'It was quite a small farm, about 150 acres, and there were just two cows for the farm's own use. Major Vaughan had been in bomb disposal in the first war.

'There were more small farmers in those days than there are now. It was mostly wheat, a bit of barley, some oats for the cattle. The wheat was mostly used for bread.'

In 1936, Bill contracted double pneumonia and had to spend six months in bed. It meant that, unlike his two brothers, he wasn't able to join the army.

'I was kept at home all the time. I had three months in isolation. I remember that the local canon at the time, Canon Edose, used to visit fairly regularly and would come and sit with me for an hour in the afternoons to relieve mother.

'He wasn't bothered about the sickness, it was his job to come and visit people. I think he was one who liked a nice little drop of drink! Mother made home-made wine in those days and it was pretty good.

'She used to make wheat wine. It was stronger than any whiskey, even a good one. It was put in a big container. There were several things that went in as well as the wheat – a potato, if I remember, then, after you'd made it and bottled it and everything, you used to have to feed it, put in a few currants and a lump of sugar. It was pretty good stuff.'

Food and other essential items were rationed in Britain from 1939 through to 1954. Bill Last's family, as with many country people, relied on food that they could produce themselves.

'Because you lived in the country, there was always a rabbit or two and you'd always got a meal. I hid my wires down by the railway line. There was always a rabbit stew pot on the hearth, that would do for a couple of days, we never went short.

'Father had a little meadow, a smallholding where he kept chickens and a couple of pigs and he'd breed the pigs. He'd save one of them and fatten it up and the Government would take half and you'd have half for your own use and they'd take one year's meat ration for it.

'We'd salt it up, take a joint or two, have some for bacon. That was hanging up in the pantry; it was an outside pantry, there was a coal shed one side and the pantry the other, it was nice and cool in there.

'It would hang up in there all year round and you could take a slice off and cook it up for breakfast, it was real bacon then, not like today. There's too much stuff put in the pigs to fatten them now.'

When Bill had recovered from his pneumonia, he went back to the farm as a tractor driver.

'When the war was over and I was well again, I moved to Manor Farm in Kelsale as a tractor driver and worked there for about 20 years. It was a bigger farm, between five and 600 acres. The Barrets gave up because the father died, they sold everything. I worked for Charles Voles. He was a Dutchman who took over Richard Barret's farm.

'I worked for him for a little while and then got wrong with him and moved down to Grove Farm, Yoxford. It was general work, I drove the tractor and helped take care of the pigs. The old man died and the daughter took over, I think I worked for them for about 30 years. I retired from there.'

In 1955, Bill married Barbara Mower.

'My wife Barbara came from Middleton. Her father Arthur had been horseman for Dan Geater on Middleton Moor. We had two boys and two girls: Patricia, Robert, Stephen and Julie.

'In the old days, we'd come into Saxmundham to the pictures two or three times a week and I'd play football.'

Christine Mattinson on Thorpeness beach with her mother and brother around 1950

Christine Mattinson b.1942

Christine Mattinson was born in South Entrance, Saxmundham, in the house now known as The Long House. Her father, Arthur Mattinson, was a well-known local tradesman and photographer. Her mother, Maisie, took care of Christine and her older brother David.

'My father was born in 1904 at Happisburgh in Norfolk. The family moved to Horsey when grandfather was appointed Rector and my father grew up sailing on the Broads. My grandfather served in the Great War as a private. After the war, the family moved to Harkstead where my great-aunts were schoolmistresses. It was there that my parents met at the local tennis club. They married in 1928 when my mother was 20.'

In 1930, Christine's parents emigrated to Canada under the Government Assisted Passenger Scheme, an incentive for British people to populate the then colony. It held great appeal for those who wanted to start a new life away from the desolating after-effects of the Great War. The Mattinsons stayed in Canada for five years. Maisie worked at a department store in Toronto, while Arthur looked for work as a motor mechanic.

It was the time of the Great Depression and, while Maisie was very happy in her job, Arthur Mattinson was unable to find work. They returned to the UK and searched for somewhere to set up on their own.

In 1938, Arthur Mattinson bought the house and business of O.W. Lane in South Entrance, Saxmundham, trading as a wireless dealer and fuel supplier.

'When war was declared in 1939, my father was rejected for enlistment on the grounds of age and poor eyesight. He was very disappointed and instead joined the Royal Observer Corps where he spent nights in the look-out post at the top of Church Hill prepared to spot incoming German planes.

'In the daytime he carried on his wireless business, helped by my mother, and also started to specialise in photography as it was difficult to get new wireless stock in during the war. My brother was born in 1940 and I was born two years later.

'My parents became friendly with a number of American Air Force personnel during the war and provided a place for them to sit and relax with a cup of tea and cake away from the base. They did not discuss their duties but I can remember mum telling me that occasionally an ambulance would be parked in the yard while the crew dropped by, giving off a strong smell of burnt flesh.

'Some friendships were maintained afterwards with correspondence between my parents and the US families. To the delight of me and my brother, they'd send us food parcels containing goodies such as sweets, gum, honey and Spam.

'My greatest childhood memory is of standing at the window in my parents' bedroom while they dressed to go out for the evening. Suddenly, there was a loud explosion on the field just along the road, followed by a noisy clanging of metal on the roof.

'A German plane was dropping bombs on Saxmundham and two had landed on the Layers, the one that scared me had landed just up the road inside the field.'

The plane was discharging bombs in order to lighten its load so that it could get home. It was the end of an unsuccessful attempt to destroy the railway in Saxmundham.

'After the war, when the USAF had gone, my parents made friends with some of the internees from Debach P.O.W. camp. The P.O.Ws worked for local farmers and had permission to spend weekends and Christmas with families as long as they reported back to camp for curfew.

'They made wooden toys like clucking hens, butterflies and a model tank for my brother. I was taken round the countryside on the crossbar of a bike and I learnt to count to ten in German with Karl tapping on the kitchen table for me to repeat after him.. eins,zwei,drei...!'

The German P.O.Ws were repatriated in 1947. Two who'd been friends of the Mattinsons returned to the Eastern zone and were never heard from again.

'My parents kept up a correspondence with the others which lasted until my mother died, and we did exchange visits with them over the years. The ironic thing was they sent us parcels of food and especially drink; and we were supposed to have won the war. One birthday my father got a stone bottle of liquid and didn't know whether it was to be drunk or used as a hair restorer!'

Christine's parents had an extraordinary willingness to open their door to those in need of friendship and support. It was at a time of many suspicions and little trust, when something as simple as a cup of tea and a slice of warm family atmosphere could make a big difference to a serviceman who was missing home. Christine has kept many of the letters that were exchanged between the servicemen and her parents.

'Father turned his car into a van for his accumulator rounds. Until then he had used a box on the back of his car. The system was that customers had two accumulators, one which they used and one spare which was collected by my father for re-charging.

'New technology was coming into the market with batteries replacing accumulators and radio replacing wireless. Television was also coming to ordinary people. Father needed space to carry the new equipment and spent a few weekends demolishing, cutting, drilling and building a new model van. My brother says that the wood and construction weighed so much he didn't think it would make it onto the road!'

The Mattinson family spent many of their weekends after the war on the River Alde at Iken, going up and down river on home-made craft, swimming and splashing around in the mud.

'One day, when we were coming back from Snape bridge to Iken, the tide was quite low and my father spotted the hull of a boat with just a bit of one side showing above the mud. He made enquiries and heard that it must have been a ship's lifeboat which had been swept off at sea and carried up river to where it had sunk.

'Having checked that no one owned it, he decided to try and retrieve it. He dug the mud out with a shovel and pick at low tide, not knowing whether the boat was damaged or not. It took several weeks but eventually he cleared the mud out and uncovered an intact hull. He then went back and attached about 30 sealed empty oil cans to the hull with short lengths of rope. We went down for the next full tide and there it was floating down the river towards us, bottom up, oil cans having lifted her. I couldn't believe my eyes.

'We retrieved her, washed her down, got her onto the trailer and took her home. Once we'd cleaned her up and checked that she was sound, father fitted her with an engine, rubbed down and painted her and named her Mudlark and returned to the water the next season for many more happy years of boating.'

Saxmundham Museum is home to the Mattinson Collection of leaflets, public notices and other printed material from the Second World War, kindly donated by the Mattinson family.

Betty Noy (2nd left) in 1952, maid of honour at her sister Mona's wedding to Peter Emsden

Betty Noy b.1931

Betty Whittaker was born in Great Yarmouth in 1931, the fourth of five children, three girls and two boys.

'I weighed 14lb, a full stone, when I was born and my mother nearly lost her life over me. She said I was up and running around on my own at six months!'

Betty's father worked as a coach manager at Watsons in Great Yarmouth. 'My grandfather drove the carriages that people could ride on along the front at Yarmouth. It was the most exciting thing in the world for a little girl, seeing my grandad go past and I used to wave at him but of course he couldn't wave back because he was working.'

When war broke out, the Whittaker family made the decision to move away from Yarmouth because of the bombing campaign which aimed to destroy the town's naval base. In 1941, Great Yarmouth was bombed intensively, with more than 100 people losing their lives.

'We tried to persuade our neighbours to come away with us but they wouldn't. In the end, their house took a direct hit and they were all killed.'

The family moved a number of times; first to Holt, then to Framlingham.

'I can remember at Framlingham it was War Weapons Week and they came to see my parents to ask if my sister Mona and I would dance for the forces stationed there. They were putting on a show at the Film Theatre. Mona and I tap danced to In the Mood and lots of other songs and cartwheeled across the stage.'

The family then moved to Kelsale, where Betty Whittaker and her siblings attended the village school.

In 1943, Betty Whittaker's parents took the licence on The Angel Inn, the former 16th-century coaching inn in the Market Place, Saxmundham. It was one of the town's most popular pubs until its closure and demolition in the 1970s.

'I left school when I was 14 and of course I had to get a job. First I worked at Maplestones [49 High Street, now the home of Saxmundham Museum]. It was a bakery and Mr Chapman used to make the bread; I started work in the shop and café at the front. The army people who were stationed at Carlton used to come in for their breakfast. It was like a little restaurant, really.'

Sadly, for 14-year-old Betty Whittaker, her first job didn't last long. 'Mr Maplestone got rid of me because customers used to come into the shop and say, "have you got any coffee?" and "have you got any chocolate?", and I would say, "yes, would you like some?" and hand it over.

'I got told off because these were things that were rationed and reserved for "special customers" and I had no business handing them out!

'I had to go home and tell my mother, who wasn't altogether pleased, and I worked at The Angel for her for five shillings a week. My sister Mona was working at home as well then. It wasn't too long before Mum came home one day and said that she'd found me a job.'

Gardener's shoe shop was a feature of Saxmundham High Street [opposite what is now the chemist and the Post Office]. The building had Gardeners at one end and a gentleman's outfitters called Daynes at the other.

Betty Whittaker worked at Gardener's shoe shop for eight years. When she married Robert Noy in 1954, she moved to Grove Farm in the Grove, Stratford St Andrew, on the Cobbold Estate. The farm had been in the Noy family for some time and Robert's father, who had been born on the farm, was still living there.

Mr Gardener wanted her to go back to her job after she was married but there was too much work to do as a farmer's wife at home. Instead, she helped train Maureen Godfrey and agreed to help at busy times and to cover holidays.

'I had to walk three miles down to the bus stop at Stratford to get the bus into Sax and three miles home from the bus stop at the end of the day because I didn't drive then.

'When the weather was bad, I'd walk from the Grove in my water boots and leave them in the hedge and put my shoes on to get to the bus stop. I did that for nine years, with no running water at the farm and no electricity. I lived down the Grove for 32 years and the only people we saw were the postman and Mr Crisp, who delivered the bread.

'It was a very hard life. I used to have to look after my father-in-law. I had to walk over three fields and do all his housework and take his dinner and go home again. There was no pleasing him with anything. It was not a happy life.'

Betty's sister Mona and Mona's husband Peter Emsden took over the licence of The Angel in 1954, just a month after Betty and Robert Noy had married.

'When I got married my parents moved to Blackburn where my elder sister lived and they took the licence on the Cemetery Hotel there. The climate didn't suit my mum, though, so Dad had to bring her back and they took The Crown on Nelson Road in Great Yarmouth. They were both glad to be back there, they were both Norfolks; dad was born in Martham, mum in Yarmouth.'

In 1957, Betty and Robert's first daughter, Jill, was born at a maternity hospital in Melton.

'Just before our second daughter Julie was born in 1963, Tony Flick came round, and he said "Betty, I wonder if the water will be on before your baby is born?" He knew that it was due to be laid on. In the end, Julie was born about three hours before the water got to us!

'People in the village bet that I'd last six months, but I've been here in Stratford for 65 years now and outlasted nearly all of them!'

We are up at dawn and we work till dusk,
sweating in the dirt and dust,
tipping corn into the bins,
out it goes to pay the bills,
cold and wet and very muddy,
we work so hard to earn our money.
Winter comes, it's cold and bleak,
time again to lift the beet,
so next time you are sitting at your table,
think of the farmers who make it all able!

Betty Noy

Acknowledgements

Most sincere thanks to everyone who agreed to be interviewed for this book. Thank you too to those who encouraged me to write More Sax Stories and those who persuaded me to carry on when I was ready to give up: Frank Bilton, Mark Fairweather, Ingrid Emsden-Fox, Peter Minta, Sandra Moore, Clare Palmier, Kyle Raynor, Penny Robertson.

Suzy Powling - editor

I don't think I would have finished this book without Suzy. We met in another age at a writers' group called Pen & Pint. I quickly identified her as someone I liked (witty) and someone who knew what she was talking about as far as writing was concerned (invaluable). She is a highly skilled professional editor. I'm so grateful that she agreed to work with me.

Printed in Great Britain
by Amazon